"Should *Asase Yaa* (Mother Earth, in Akan) decide to speak today, her voice would reverberate with the sounds contained in *Preaching Black Earth*. The authors of this polyphonic and polyvocal anthology witness through interviews, poems, spoken word, and preaching the groaning, sighing, and loud expressions of the agonies and triumphs of Mother Earth. The editor of this exceptional work, Professor Melanie Harris, has truly allowed the earth to have being and voice and thus be a participant in the global struggle for justice. Not only is God's creative vision that all beings live in harmony clearly declared in this volume, but also ways of teaching, preaching, and creatively modeling the vision are made abundantly clear."

—Emmanuel Y. Lartey, Charles Howard Candler Professor of Pastoral Theology and Spiritual Care, Candler School of Theology, Emory University

"*Preaching Black Earth* spurs our theological imagination for what it means to live in fidelity with the wider creation. This volume is thoughtful, inspiring, and adept in its attention to culture and contexts. Harris has curated another compelling collection that elevates Black women's spiritual wisdom as a vital source for engaging our daily encounters as opportunities for sacred practice. Practitioners, laity, and scholars alike will consider this a must for their personal libraries."

—Lisa L. Thompson, Associate Professor and Cornelius Vanderbilt Chair in Black Homiletics and Liturgics, Vanderbilt University

"This exquisite, spirit-filled, anthology invites all readers to centralize ecowomanist insights and methods in our work for earth justice. This book is a crucial guide for environmental and social justice in these times, especially (but not only) in North America. And the time to listen is now—especially for those of us of settler-colonial descent who inherited white theological privilege."

—Christiana Zenner, Associate Professor of Theology, Science, and Ethics at Fordham University

"The brilliance and prophetic wisdom that mark Melanie Harris's work abound in this book. It is a wellspring of deeply rooted soul-sustenance for the uncharted journey toward a world where Earth and earthlings may flourish. Ecowomanist wisdom guides the reader to weave contemplative practice into transformative power for earth justice as social justice. Brave and tender words light the way. Drink from this luminous volume to water your soul, illumine your connection to all that is, and ignite enduring courage for the collective sacred work of ecological social healing that is the great spiritual and moral calling of our time in history."

—Cynthia Moe-Lobeda, Professor of Theology and Social Ethics at Church Divinity School of the Pacific and author of *Resisting Structural Evil: Love as Ecological-Economic Vocation*; *Building a Moral Economy: Pathways for People of Courage*; and other works

"This text brings together leading academicians, activists, and religious leaders who care about justice for people and the earth and shows how justice for people and justice for the earth are intimately connected. Bringing together the wisdom from environmental justice, earth justice, ecowomanism, and liberation and black theologies among others, the sermons, interviews, and poems in this book help us to look at the intersectional issues involved in eco-injustice faced by peoples, nonhuman life, and the planetary community. Most importantly, the writings in this text not only appeal to our rational selves but also appeal to the deep affective realities that lie in the wake of colonization, slavery, and ecological degradation."

—Whitney A. Bauman, Professor, Religious Studies,
Florida International University

"This book is powerful in ways that deserve both careful attention and enduring praise. The variety of voices represented here is stunning. They are drawn together with Melanie's skilled weaving of suffering, solace, and solidarity in our times. She invites us into the space of effective transformative action."

—Mary Evelyn Tucker, Codirector, Yale Forum on Religion and Ecology

Preaching Black Earth

Preaching Black Earth

*Sermons, Meditations, and Conversations
on African American Environmental Justice
and Ecowomanist Spirituality*

Edited by Melanie L. Harris

WESTMINSTER
JOHN KNOX PRESS
LOUISVILLE · KENTUCKY

© 2025 Westminster John Knox Press

First edition
Published by Westminster John Knox Press
Louisville, Kentucky

25 26 27 28 29 30 31 32 33 34—10 9 8 7 6 5 4 3 2 1

All rights reserved. No part of this book may be reproduced or transmitted in any form or by any means, electronic or mechanical, including photocopying, recording, or by any information storage or retrieval system, without permission in writing from the publisher. For information, address Westminster John Knox Press, 100 Witherspoon Street, Louisville, Kentucky 40202-1396. Or contact us online at www.wjkbooks.com.

Scripture quotations marked NIV are from The Holy Bible, New International Version®. Copyright © 1973, 1978, 1984, 2011 by Biblica, Inc.® Used with permission of Zondervan. All rights reserved worldwide. www.zondervan.com

Scripture quotations marked NLT are taken from the Holy Bible, New Living Translation, copyright 1996, 2004. Used by permission of Tyndale House Publishers, Inc., Wheaton, Illinois 60189. All rights reserved.

Scripture quotations from the ESV® Bible (The Holy Bible, English Standard Version®), © 2001 by Crossway, a publishing ministry of Good News Publishers. Used by permission. All rights reserved.

Rachel Elizabeth Harding, "Daughter's Précis," in *Remnants: A Memoir of Spirit, Activism, and Mothering* by Rosemarie Freeney Harding, pp. ix–xxiv. Copyright 2015, Duke University Press. All rights reserved. Republished by permission of the copyright holder, and the Publisher. www.dukeupress.edu.

Stacey Abrams's sermon "Stewardship, Service, and Redemption" is reprinted with permission from Stacey Abrams. Sofía Betancourt's sermon "Transcendentalism and the Harrowed Black Earth" is reprinted with permission from Sofía Betancourt. Elonda Clay's sermon "Exodus in a Warming World" is reprinted with permission from Elonda Clay. John W. Kinney's sermon "Collapsing the Hierarchy" is reprinted with permission from John W. Kinney. Otis Moss's sermon "By Any Greens Necessary" is reprinted with permission from Otis Moss III. Kenneth Ngwa's sermon "Rocky, Earthy Dreams" is reprinted with permission from Kenneth Ngwa. Liv Parsons's poem "You Can't Shift the Stars" is reprinted with permission from Liv Parsons.

Book design by Sharon Adams
Cover design by Geronna Lewis-Lyte

Library of Congress Cataloging-in-Publication Data is on file
at the Library of Congress, Washington, DC.

ISBN: 978-0-664-26836-7

Most Westminster John Knox Press books are available at special quantity discounts when purchased in bulk by corporations, organizations, and special-interest groups. For more information, please e-mail SpecialSales@wjkbooks.com.

To John Asante Arberia Harris
you are loved
the echo of stars lives in you
ancestors' smiles are reborn in your heart every day
you breathe
in
strength
pray earth joy, justice and sorrow
god will meet you
see yourself true
free
whole
earth love, earth prayers
are holding you
even
now
mama loves you

Table of Contents

Acknowledgments   ix

Introduction: Preaching, Teaching, Leading, and Writing for Climate Justice
   MELANIE L. HARRIS   1

Poem: breathing earth   18
   MELANIE L. HARRIS

Part I: Earth Wisdom, Word, and Active Compassion: Ecowomanist Sermons and Meditations
   MELANIE L. HARRIS   19

1. Stewardship, Service, and Redemption: Called to Be God's Ministers
   STACEY ABRAMS   23

2. Exodus in a Warming World: An Ecowomanist Sermon
   ELONDA CLAY   33

3. Rocky, Earthy Dreams
   KENNETH NGWA   51

4. Transcendentalism and the Harrowed Black Earth
   SOFÍA BETANCOURT   57

5. Collapsing the Hierarchy
   JOHN W. KINNEY   63

6. By Any Greens Necessary
   OTIS MOSS III   67

Poem: release
   MELANIE L. HARRIS   72

Part II: Earth Heart, Earth Hope: Conversations on African American Environmental Justice and Ecowomanist Spirituality
MELANIE L. HARRIS   73

7. Ecowomanist Prophetic Voices: Black Liberation Theology and a Vision of Earth Resurrection
INTERVIEW WITH FREDERICK DOUGLASS HAYNES III   81

8. Ecowomanist Spirituality: Earth Home and Homiletics
INTERVIEW WITH GINA M. STEWART   91

9. Ecowomanist Community: Antiracism, Love, and Justice
INTERVIEW WITH LARRY RASMUSSEN   101

10. Ecowomanist Leadership: Black Women, Freedom, and Environmental Justice
INTERVIEW WITH CHRISTOPHER CARTER AND HEBER BROWN III   119

11. "Loves . . . Roundness" Ecowomanist Shape, Theory, and Method
A CONVERSATION WITH KATE COMMON, MELANIE L. HARRIS, AND FRANCES ROBERTS-GREGORY   137

Poem: You Can't Shift the Stars
LIV PARSONS   155

Poem: earth speaks
MELANIE L. HARRIS   158

Conclusion: Engaging Contemplative Thought, Ethics, and Practice
MELANIE L. HARRIS   161

Contributors   181

Index   187

Acknowledgments

Writing is an art form that invites friends. From the grace of the redwood trees in California to the laughter of children sharing their own hopes for preaching with earth, I have been gifted by many on this journey for whom I am deeply grateful. I want to express gratitude to my mother, Rev. Dr. Naomi O. Harris, for her fortitude in faith, deep love, and wisdom. Thank you, Mom, for pouring into me such deep spiritual power and love such that I feel anchored in Spirit. Always. My brother, John Arberia Harris Jr., and his family are sources of strength and encouragement for me. It is a gift to share this life journey with you; thank you. The ancestral spirit of my father, John A. Harris Sr., meets me with the sun every morning. Thank you, Daddy. Your smile surrounds me. I see you. The gift of parenting is a precious grace. Thank you, John Asante A. Harris, for being in my life. Loving you is the greatest gift my heart has ever known. I love you, and I am very proud of you.

Family love and support have carried me since before I was born. I want to thank the Harris, Perry, Wells, Turner, Jones, Jackson, and Dozier families for the ways they have prayed for me and my writing journey. Special thanks to Hattie Mae Patterson, Clara Turner Beamon, Premilee Reed Turner, Vicki Perry Dennis, Stephanie Perry Fisher, Gloria Perry, Tracey Jackson and Kent Jackson and family, and Sonia Denise, Keith, Alisha, Nathan, and Desmond Dozier for their deep prayers and presence.

Spirit has blessed me with a remarkable family beyond blood that has helped me give birth to myself again and again as I deepened in my writing path and spiritual calling. I would like to thank Alice Walker for sharing beautiful wisdom with me and keeping me attuned always to the gift of revolutionary writing and earth justice. Mama A, thank you. You are cherished and deeply loved. Caroline Odeji, thank you for being a spiritual mother and for teaching me the sacred gifts of discernment. My Santa Fe parents, Larry and Nyla Rasmussen have been midwives for my writing journey since my early days as a graduate student at Union Theological Seminary in the City of New York. Thank you always for keeping hope in your hearts for me and creating such a bountiful life of love for your children and grandchildren. We love you.

True friendship creates room in the heart that enhances strength through vulnerability. I am blessed to have many friends and colleagues in the work of justice. Many of the contributors in this volume are also cherished mentors and friends. I thank Stacey Abrams, Rev. Dr. Sofia Betancourt, Rev. Dr. Heber Brown III, Rev. Dr. Christopher Carter, Elonda Clay, Dr. Kate Common, Rev. Dr. Otis Moss III, Rev. Dr. Kenneth Ngwa, Dr. Larry Rasmussen, Liv Parsons, and Dr. Frances Roberts-Gregory. I especially thank Rev. Dr. Frederick Douglass Haynes III for his incredible support of my work and ministry, Rev. Dr. John Kinney for his mentoring wisdom and love, and Rev. Dr. Gina M. Stewart for her incredible gifts as a pastor, leader, and activist around the world.

I would also like to thank many friends for their gifted presence on this writing journey: Rev. Dr. Stephanie Crumpton , Dr. Nikki Hoskins, Rev. Dr. Jennifer Leath, Rev. Dr. Eboni Turman Marshall, Rev. Cheryl Walker, Elizabeth Terry, Hilary Hart, Sophie Ivey, Sally Mirana, Zoe Gamell Brown, the Sister Tree Sisters Writing Group, Rev. Dr. Willie Jennings, Dr. Cynthia Moe Lobeda, Rev. Dr. Michelle Lewis, A. W. Shields, Shilpa Jain, Dr. Sonya Shah, Rev. Damien Durr, Rev. Dr. Emmanuel Lartey, Rev. Dr. Joretta Marshall, Joy Allen, Dana Marshall, Mark Nelson Sr. and family, Rev. Wesley Morris, Kenya Morris, Rev. Talitha Arnold, Rev. Dr. Kenya Ayers, Dr. Norman Wirzba, Dr. Carolyn Finney, Dr. Michael Ebeling, Eric and Meghan Flow, Jean Marie Brown, Dr. Claire Sanders, Dr. Fran Huckaby, Tyrone, LaShica and Kaj Beverly, Dr. Rachel Harding, Myra Donovan, Patricia Raybon, Dr. Charles Hallisey, Dr. Janet Gyatso, Professor John Brown, Dr. Pamela Ayo Yetunde, Sister Peace, Dr. Cheryl Giles, Dr. Jan Willis, Rev. Dr. Leslie Callahan, Dr. Iva Carruthers, Dr. Michelle Chatmann, Dr. Layli Maparyan, Dr. Julie Valesquez-Runk, Dr. Justin Wolfe and the Social Distance Writing Group, Doug and Cathy Drabble, Dr. Keri Day, Dr. Brooke Dodson-Lavelle, Cheryl Fairbanks, Dr. Cari Jackson, Dr. Felita Johnson, Rev. Lisa Lynne Kirkpatrick, Dr. April Ruffin-Adams, Kaira Jewel Lingo, Joseph, Bridget and Imani Belyeu, Mary Luker and Kimberly Robinson, Kate Mosley, Adrienne Numaworse, Dr. Tina Pippin, Dr. Hilary Smith, Dr. Terry Tempest Williams, Dr. Chanequa Walker-Barnes, and Dr. Christiana Zenner.

Several faith communities and organizations committed to the development of ecowomanist spiritualty and environmental justice provided institutional, intellectual, spiritual and financial support to complete this project. I thank the Samuel DeWitt Proctor Conference; the Kalliopeia Foundation; Faith Community Church in the City of Greensboro, North Carolina; Christ Missionary Baptist Church in Memphis, Tennessee; Ebenezer Baptist Church in Beaverdam, Virginia; the Barre Center for Buddhist Studies;

the Wabash Center for Teaching and Learning in Theology and Religion; Agnes Scott College; Wake Forest School of Divinity and Wake Forest University; Candler School of Theology at Emory University; the Ahimsa Collective; the Root Cause Collective; the Ecowomanist Center in Research, Climate Justice, Leadership, and the Environment; the Winston-Salem Chapter of Jack and Jill America Inc.; and the Dharma Care Sangha Sisters.

Special thanks to Dr. Bridgett Green for her incredible care, sharp editing genius, and thoughtfulness. It is a gift to have an editor who moves with a spirit of excellence. Thank you. I would also like to thank Daniel Braden and the entire publishing team at Westminster John Knox Press. Ancestors, thank you. Spirit's guidance, restoration, deep love, and prayer have shaped this journey into being. I am grateful. May we all cherish earth, seek justice, and work toward wholeness for all beings.

Introduction

Preaching, Teaching, Leading, and Writing for Climate Justice

MELANIE L. HARRIS

Coming to voice together for the sake of earth justice is the purpose of this book. *Preaching Black Earth* is a collection of meditations, sermons, and interviews from scholars, preachers, and leading spiritual activists in the environmental justice movement that connect the prophetic tradition of spoken word, prophetic truth telling, contemplative thought, ecowomanism, and homiletics in the historical Black church with the environment. While it features many different homiletical styles, the book is not a traditional text in African American preaching that focuses on sermon development. Rather it is an interdisciplinary text that features models of earth-honoring faith and biblically inspired sermons. It is evidence of the importance of intellectual community, collaboration, and sharing of thought as art. When mutual enhancement, environmental justice, and ecological reparations are the goals, then the conversation between thinkers, scholars, and activists looks different. It is collaborative, not competitive. It leans into truth and community building, not reestablishing, falling prey to, or being complicit in hierarchical relationship. It is interdisciplinary, intersectional, and includes multiple fields connected to environmental studies and committed to environmental justice.[1]

The interdisciplinary and intersectional frame of ecowomanism guides this volume and helps us as readers to see the many different sides or perspectives within environmental justice. Ecowomanism is an approach to environmental ethics and studies that uses intersectional (race, class, gender, sexuality, ability) analysis and centers the voices, contributions, and methods of women of

---

1. For more on mutual enhancement, see Melanie L. Harris, "In the Company of Friends: Womanist Readings of Buddhist Poems," *Buddhist-Christian Studies* 36 (2016): 3–8.

color, especially women of African descent. Naming the importance of these women's approaches to climate justice as key to ecological reparations and strategies for moving us toward climate justice, ecowomanism both uncovers the his/herstory of women of African descent in the environmental movement and debunks the myth that the environment is a "white people's issue."[2]

Applying an ecowomanist lens provides a fresh lens to environmental justice in that it reveals the interdisciplinary, intersecting and intercultural, and interfaith perspectives that flow from critically exploring climate justice from a variety of perspectives. All these perspectives are necessary for the facing of this hour on the planet and the deep challenges that climate change means for the human and nonhuman earth community. One of the primary tenets of ecowomanist thought is the interconnected lens of justice. That is, for ecowomanism social justice is earth justice and earth justice is social justice. Put another way, social justice issues, including racism, classism, sexism, heterosexism, ableism, and other unjust forms of oppressions, are important to take into consideration when examining environmental justice.

So, what is environmental justice? Environmental justice is the work of justice for earth and all beings on the earth. It especially honors the voices of communities of color and reveals the intersections between racial, gender, economic, and social injustice in connection with policy making decisions that place marginalized communities further at risk of being treated unfairly in society and trapped in unhealthy environments due to air pollution, soil contamination, overuse and unfair use of land, and more. According to Dorceta E. Taylor, "The environmental justice movement arose because of the urgent need to make connections between racism, discrimination, equity, justice, and the environment."[3] Recognizing the importance of interconnectedness between all beings for many in Indigenous cultural and religious communities and woven into many spiritual communities of people of color, the term "earth justice" is also used to describe work in the environmental justice movement that includes the voice of earth. Earth justice acknowledges the agency of nonhuman beings and offers a frame through which to think about how to create environmental justice that includes the earth. It takes seriously the voices of earth, wind, fire, and water—the ancestral message that the earth is speaking especially regarding the disappearance of certain forms of biodiversity on the planet, the erasure of certain plant species, and the unjust killing of too many people, animals, and trees for the sake of domination and human greed.

---

2. Alice Walker, "Nuclear Madness," in *In Search of Our Mothers' Gardens: Womanist Prose* (Harcourt Brace Jovanovich, 1983), 345.

3. Dorceta E. Taylor, "Environmental Justice Demands Listening," *Sierra*, accessed February 27, 2024, https://digital.sierramagazine.org/publication/?i=686367&article_id=3841577&view=articleBrowser.